Rivers of the World

Susan Brocker

PowerKiDS
press

New York

Published in 2009 by The Rosen Publishing Group, Inc.
29 East 21st Street, New York, NY 10010

Consultant: Colin Sale
U.S. Editor: Erin Heath

Photo Credits: Cover, title page © DEA/R. Carnovalini/Getty Images; pp. 5, 7, 10–11, 20–21, 23–25, 26–27 (bottom) Photobank Image Library; pp. 9, 22 Minden Pictures/Stock Image Group; p. 11 (top) The Mariners' Museum: Newport News, VA; pp. 12–13 Mary Evans Picture Library; pp. 18–19, 27 (top), 29 Tranz/Corbis; p. 28 Rolf and Debra Kraiker; p. 30, 31 (top) stockxpert

Illustration Credits: All illustrations © Weldon Owen Inc.

Library of Congress Cataloging-in-Publication Data

Brocker, Susan, 1961–
  Rivers of the world / Susan Brocker.
      p. cm. — (Our planet)
  Includes index.
  ISBN 978-1-4358-2816-2 (library binding)
  1. Rivers—Juvenile literature. I. Title.
  GB1203.8.B75 2009
  551.48'3—dc22

                              2008034746

Printed in Malaysia

Contents

A River's Journey 4

Shaping the Land 6

Rivers of Life 8

People and Rivers 10

Exploring Africa 12

Great Rivers of the World 14

A Tale of Two Rivers

The Nile River 16

The Amazon River 18

Life Along a River 20

Using Rivers Today 22

Power from a River 24

Change with Care 26

Fun on the River 28

Glossary 30

Index and Web Sites 32

A River's Journey

Rivers carry the freshwater needed for life on Earth. A river usually starts high in the mountains. The **source** can be an underground spring, an area with heavy rainfall, or melting snow on a mountain. As a river flows downhill, it is joined by other streams, called **tributaries**. It ends at a **mouth**, where it flows into a lake or an ocean.

A river usually first tumbles down steep hills, rushing over rocks and waterfalls. As the land flattens, a river slows and winds gently through valleys and plains.

Rivers have three sections. The upper course flows quickly. The middle course winds along valleys. The lower course joins into a lake or a sea.

1 Source
2 Upper course
3 Middle course
4 Tributary
5 Lower course
6 Mouth

The Ganges

Many people think that rivers are special places. The Ganges River in India is sacred to Hindu people. Many Hindus travel from around the world to bathe in the river.

Shaping the Land

Running water is very powerful. Over millions of years, rivers wear down Earth's surface, carving out deep valleys and carrying away rock. When tiny pieces of rock build up around seas and lakes, plains of rich soil are formed for use as farmland.

A river can also change the land quickly. Heavy rain or melting snow can cause a river to swell and flood the surrounding land in just a few hours. Sometimes a flood can cause a river to burst its banks and completely change direction.

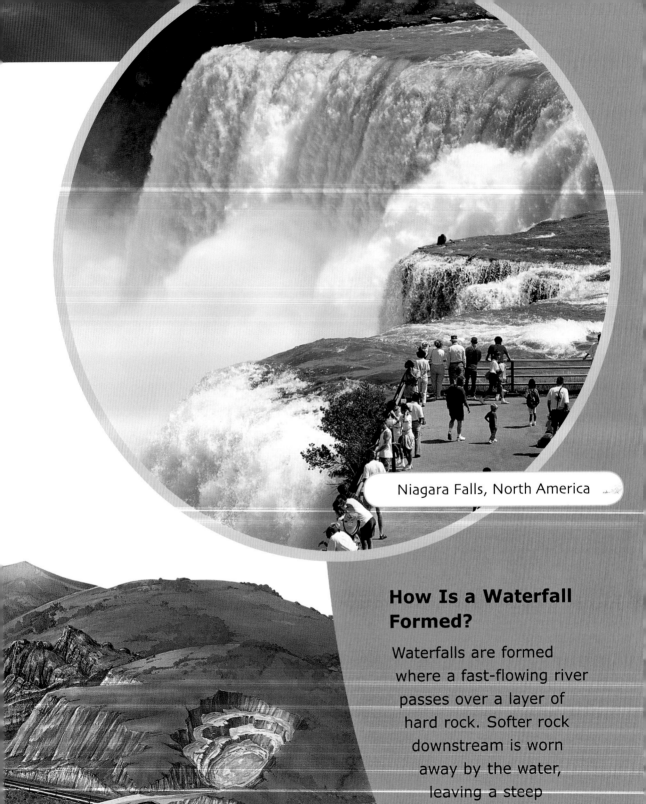

Niagara Falls, North America

How Is a Waterfall Formed?

Waterfalls are formed where a fast-flowing river passes over a layer of hard rock. Softer rock downstream is worn away by the water, leaving a steep drop over which the water plunges.

7

Rivers of Life

A river is home to many different plants and animals. Some, such as tiny algae and fish, live in the water. Plants grow well along a riverbank, and many kinds of animals come down to the river to drink, feed, and bathe.

Different plants and animals are found in different parts of a river. Fish such as salmon are strong swimmers that live in fast-flowing parts of the river. In slow-moving waters, plants such as water lilies can grow well.

FAST FACT

A Mighty Journey

Salmon hatch in pools near the sources of some fast-flowing rivers. They swim downstream and then out to sea but return to lay eggs in the same part of the river where they hatched. They swim upstream and across **rapids**, using their sense of smell to find "home."

Bears in Alaska and Canada are quick and strong. They can easily snatch a salmon from a fast-flowing river.

People and Rivers

For thousands of years, people have settled beside rivers. Rivers provide freshwater for drinking, cooking, and washing. The rich land along a river is often ideal for farming.

In the past, traveling by river was often the quickest and easiest way to explore new lands. Many famous explorers followed rivers. As business between towns increased, rivers became important highways for moving goods on boats and barges.

Saint Lawrence River, Canada

Canada

Saint Lawrence River

Gulf of Saint Lawrence

CANADA

Lake Ontario

UNITED STATES

NORTH ATLANTIC OCEAN

Jacques Cartier

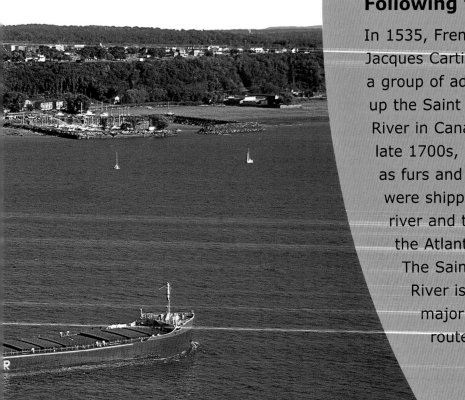

Following the River

In 1535, French explorer Jacques Cartier led a group of adventurers up the Saint Lawrence River in Canada. By the late 1700s, goods such as furs and wood were shipped down the river and then across the Atlantic Ocean. The Saint Lawrence River is still a major shipping route today.

Exploring Africa

Mary Henrietta Kingsley (1862–1900) was a British explorer. She traveled to unmapped parts of Africa in 1893 and 1894.

Not much is known about her first visit, but her second visit began at the mouth of the Ogowé River, in Gabon, Africa. Kingsley traveled by canoe up the river to explore parts of forest not yet seen by a European. She collected bugs, shells, fish, and plants for the British Museum.

In 1899, Kingsley left for South Africa to collect fish from the Orange River. However, she arrived in Cape Town just as a war began. She helped nurse prisoners until she caught a fever in the prison camp. She died in June 1900 and was buried at sea.

Mary Kingsley

Africa

Niger River

Mount Cameroon

AFRICA

Lake Ncovi

ATLANTIC OCEAN

Ogowé River

Congo River

It was at Lake Ncovi that Kingsley first saw a group of gorillas. She later wrote, "I have seen many wild animals in their native wilds, but never have I seen anything to equal gorillas going through the bush; it is a graceful, powerful, superbly perfect hand-trapeze performance."

In Africa, Kingsley wore dresses with layers and layers of petticoats. When she fell 15 feet (5 m) into a game pit filled with sharp spikes, she lived to tell the story. "It is at these times you realize the blessing of a good, thick skirt," she said.

After being rescued from the game pit, Kingsley returned to her canoe. A hippopotamus was waiting at the river, and "after scratching him behind the ear with my umbrella, we parted 'friends.'"

Traveling up the Ogowé River

Great Rivers of the World

Saint Lawrence River

- Carries more freight than any other Canadian river
- Connects the Atlantic Ocean and the Great Lakes

Colorado River

- Carved out the Grand Canyon
- Supplies water to seven states in the United States and to Mexico

Mississippi River

- Main shipping river of the United States
- Name comes from a Native American word for "the big river"

Amazon River

- Second-longest river in the world
- Carries more water than any other river
- Is up to 6 miles (10 km) wide for most of its length

Greenland

ARCTIC OCEAN

Canada

NORTH AMERICA

EUROPE

ATLANTIC OCEAN

AFRICA

SOUTH AMERICA

River Thames

- England's most important river
- Flows through the heart of London past many famous buildings

Nile River

- Longest river in the world
- Was important for the ancient Egyptians, and people still use it today

Yangtze River

- Third-longest river in the world
- Home to China's rare whitefin river dolphin

Murray River

- Longest river in Australia
- Necessary source of water for crops

Zambezi River

- Plunges over Victoria Falls
- Is the border between two African countries

Ganges River

- India's longest river
- Sacred to Hindu people
- Forms the world's largest **delta**

ASIA

India

China

PACIFIC OCEAN

INDIAN OCEAN

AUSTRALIA

A Tale of Two Rivers

The world's two largest rivers flow through very different land areas. The Nile is the longest river on Earth. It flows through the dry desert of northern Africa. The Amazon is the world's biggest river. It carries the most water and flows through a huge rain forest in South America.

The Nile River

Ancient Egyptians lived along the banks of the Nile and built great buildings such as graves and temples along its shores. The people used the river for drinking and for **irrigating** their crops.

Egypt

Mediterranean Sea

EGYPT

Nile River

SAUDI ARABIA

Red Sea

SUDAN

ETHIOPIA

CONGO

KENYA

INDIAN OCEAN

Ancient Egyptians Farming the Shores of the Nile River

Seeds were thrown onto the moist soil and plowed using animals.

Every villager worked during harvesttime. Men cut the crop with blades. Women separated the grain.

A bucket and weight device called a shaduf was used to lift water from the Nile.

The Amazon River

Many native groups live along the Amazon River. They fish in the wide river and hunt in the forest.

The Amazon is also home for a great amount of wildlife. There are more than 2,000 kinds of fish in the Amazon River, including the flesh-eating piranha. The world's biggest snake, the anaconda, also spends most of its life in the Amazon River. Some lily pads in the Amazon grow up to 3 feet (1 m) wide. Each pad grows big and strong enough to hold the weight of a child.

Amazon Basin

ATLANTIC OCEAN

Amazon River

Piranha

WORD BUILDER

In 1541, the Spanish explorer Francisco de Orellana traveled up the Amazon River. He said he was attacked by a band of women with bows and arrows. He called them Amazons, like the fierce female warriors of Greek myth. This was how the river got its name.

Life Along a River

The Mississippi, together with its main tributary, the Missouri, forms the greatest river system in North America. For centuries, the river was an important trading route for Native Americans. Later, it was the pathway for European settlement in the United States. From the early 1800s, steamboats took settlers and goods up and down the river.

The Mississippi curls through hills, down through the plains, and to the **bayous** of the South. Many people have settled along its banks, creating an exciting mix of groups and ways of life.

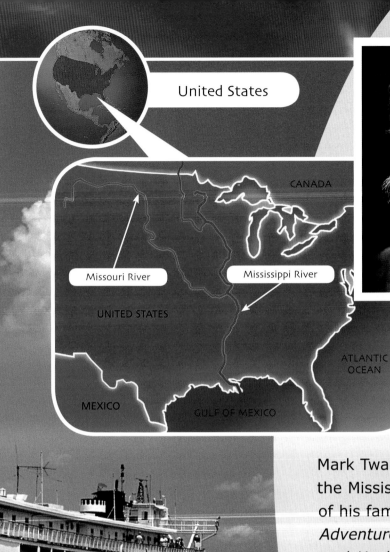

United States

CANADA

Missouri River

Mississippi River

UNITED STATES

ATLANTIC OCEAN

MEXICO

GULF OF MEXICO

Mark Twain
1835–1910

Mark Twain grew up beside the Mississippi River. Two of his famous stories, *The Adventures of Tom Sawyer* and *Huckleberry Finn,* were set by the river. He was born Samuel Clemens but changed his name to Mark Twain after working as a steamboat pilot. Pilots called out "Mark Twain!" while checking the depth of the river. It meant the river was two fathoms deep, or about 12 feet (4 m).

Using Rivers Today

Many towns and cities around the world get their water supply directly from rivers. As well as drinking, cooking, and washing with it, people use river water to manufacture goods and produce electricity.

Some factories need huge amounts of water for cleaning and mixing products. If they use river water to flush away waste materials, it can cause river pollution.

Even with today's many roads and rails, rivers are still used to ship goods. Tugs and boats move heavy freight cheaply and quickly. In the countryside, farmers channel river water into ditches, canals, and sprinklers to irrigate their fields. In some cities, people live on rivers in houseboats.

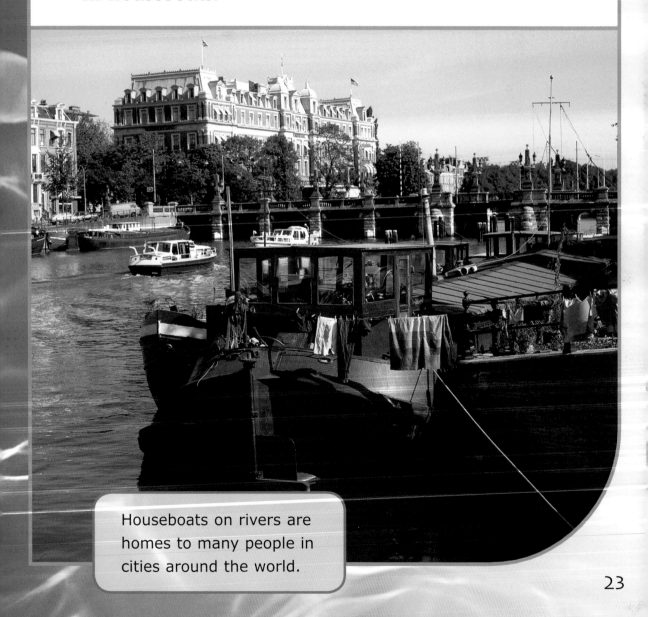

Houseboats on rivers are homes to many people in cities around the world.

Power from a River

In the past, people used the power of running water in fast-flowing rivers to turn waterwheels. Waterwheels powered simple machines such as grinders and hammers.

Today, we use rivers to make electricity by turning huge waterwheels called turbines. A dam is built across a river to hold back the water. When the dam gates are opened, water rushes through a tunnel and hits the turbines. The force of the water spins the turbines to make electricity. This is called **hydroelectric power**.

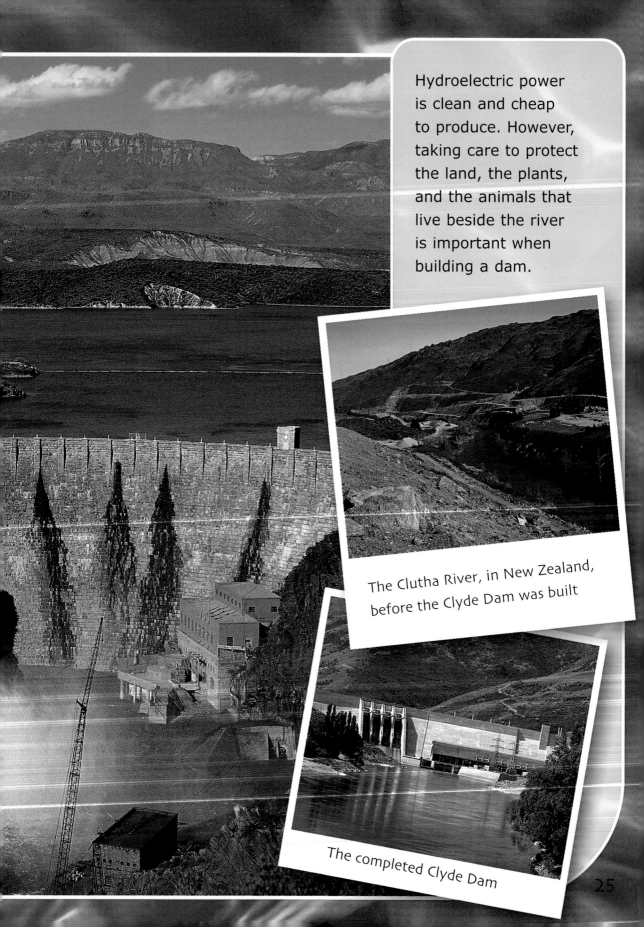

Hydroelectric power is clean and cheap to produce. However, taking care to protect the land, the plants, and the animals that live beside the river is important when building a dam.

The Clutha River, in New Zealand, before the Clyde Dam was built

The completed Clyde Dam

Change with Care

People have used and changed rivers for hundreds of years. They've built dams and banks to stop flooding. They've built canals and **aqueducts** to move water. They've straightened rivers and built **locks** to help move goods. People have even drained rivers to provide more land.

People have also changed rivers by polluting them. Today, people in many places are learning that it is important to care for rivers.

River Thames, England

Cleaning the Connecticut

The Connecticut River was once the most polluted river in the United States. Some parts ran red with dyes from factories. In 1972, people began river cleanups. Now salmon are returning, and the river is clean and beautiful again.

Fun on the River

Rivers are also fun! People enjoy swimming and fishing from the banks of rivers. Some people row, sail, or cruise along slow-moving rivers. Other people take on fast-flowing rivers by "shooting the rapids" in boats and rafts.

Rivers are often beautiful places to visit for a walk, a picnic, or seeing wildlife. Some have cool features such as plunging waterfalls and white-water rapids.

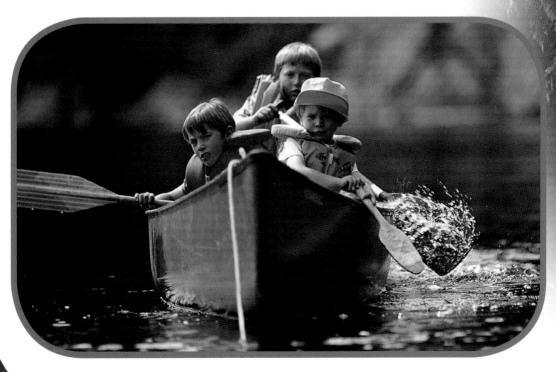

A slow-moving river is an ideal place to learn how to paddle a canoe.

Which River Is Safe?

Rivers are graded on a scale of 1 to 6. Grade 1 rivers have little or no current and no big rocks or holes. Grade 6 rivers are very dangerous, with large drops over waterfalls and huge rocks. They are usually thought to be impossible for any activity, or "unrunnable," even by experts.

Glossary

aqueduct (A-kweh-dukt) A pipe
or a channel built for moving water
across long distances.

bayou (BY-oo) A word used mainly in
the South to describe a stream that runs
through wet, marshy areas. It runs from
or into a larger river or a lake.

delta (DEL-tuh) An area of land built
out into a sea or a lake. A delta forms
a triangle shape where the flow of a river
stops and mud, sand, or rock are dropped.

hydroelectric power
(hy-droh-ih-LEK-trik POW-ur)
Power that is produced by the
force of running water.

irrigating (IR-uh-gayt-ing) Bringing water to the land by using pipes, sprinklers, and ditches. In some areas where there is little rain, farmers use the water from nearby rivers to irrigate their fields.

lock (LOK) An enclosed part of a river with gates built at each end so that boats can be lifted or lowered to different sections of the river.

mouth (MOWTH) The place where a river enters a sea or a lake.

rapids (RA-pidz) Parts of a river where the water flows very quickly over rocks.

source (SORS) The beginning of a stream or a river.

tributary (TRIH-byuh-ter-ee) A stream or a river that flows into a larger river.

Index

Africa	12–16
Amazon River	14, 16, 18–19
Cartier, Jacques	11
Colorado River	14
Connecticut River	27
fish	8–9, 18–19
Ganges River	5, 15
hydroelectric power	24–25
Kingsley, Mary	12–13
Mississippi River	14, 20–21
Murray River	15
Nile River	15–17
Ogowé River	12–13
Orellana, Francisco de	19
plants	8, 18
pollution	22, 26–27
Saint Lawrence River	10–11, 14
Thames, River	15, 26
waterfalls	7, 28–29
Yangtze River	15
Zambezi River	15

Web Sites

Due to the changing nature of Internet links, PowerKids Press has developed an online list of Web sites related to the subject of this book. This site is updated regularly. Please use this link to access the list:

www.powerkidslinks.com/opla/river/